BOTERO

in the
MUSEO NACIONAL
DE COLOMBIA

New donation 2004

BOTERO

in the
MUSEO NACIONAL
DE COLOMBIA
New donation 2004

Direction, design and edition
BENJAMÍN VILLEGAS

Texts
BEATRIZ GONZÁLEZ
SANTIAGO LONDOÑO VÉLEZ

Introduction
ELVIRA CUERVO DE JARAMILLO

Photography
J. HYDE
MUSEO NACIONAL ARCHIVES
VILLEGAS EDITORES

Villegas
editores

This book-catalogue has been created,
produced and published in Colombia by
VILLEGAS EDITORES
Avenida 82 No. 11-50, Interior 3
Bogotá, D.C., Colombia.
Telephone (57-1) 616 1788
Fax (57-1) 616 0020
e-mail: informacion@VillegasEditores.com

Editorial Asistant
MARÍA VILLEGAS

Art Department
ENRIQUE CORONADO

English Translation
JIMMY WEISKOPF

First edition, May 2004

ISBN, 958-8156-49-1

Cover and back cover,
Massacre in Colombia, 2000.
Oil on canvas, 129 x 192 cm

Page 2,
The procession (detail), 2000.
Oil on canvas, 191 x 128 cm

Page 5,
Death in the Catedral (detail), 2002.
Oil on canvas, 196 x 131 cm

Page 6,
Massacre in Colombia (detail), 2000.
Oil on canvas, 129 x 192 cm

Page 8,
Massacre in the Ciénaga Grande (detail), 2001
Oil on canvas, 157 x 200 cm

Color selection
ZETTA COMUNICADORES

Printed in Colombia by
PANAMERICANA FORMAS E IMPRESOS S. A.

VillegasEditores.com

Introduction

With the following words, published in the *Revista Diners* (Diners Magazine) in February 2000, Fernando Botero announced the biggest donation given by a Colombian artist to the museums of his country up to then: "... the pleasure I feel in doing something for my country is much, much greater than the regret that might arise from parting company with these works. I am delighted to do it. The time has come to show these pictures in Colombia, so that people can look at and enjoy them."

At that time, the donation consisted of his own paintings and drawings and an important collection of international art that was divided between Bogotá and Medellín. Nevertheless, philanthropy has been a constant feature in the career of this painter. Public institutions, like the National Museum of Colombia, have benefited from his generosity several times, which has enabled them to build up their collections of his work.

Botero has stated on various occasions that, although he has not lived in Colombia for more than forty years, he feels very close to what is happening here and is concerned about the crisis that the nation faces. Convinced that expressions of solidarity should be made when the country most needs them, he has confirmed his commitment to its cultural institutions once again with the donation of 27 drawings and 23 oil paintings to the collection of the National Museum of Colombia.

By means of this gesture, Botero has proved once more that he is not only an example to other artists but to all Colombians who can contribute to the growth of the cultural heritage of the country with their generosity.

This new collection will enrich the collections of the National Museum in an extraordinary manner and help future generations to reach an understanding of the harsh, painful and incomprehensible situation which Colombians have endured for many years.

Maestro Botero justifiably thought that this series of works should never be commercialized and for this reason they may only belong to the Colombian people and be exhibited in the Museum that belongs to all of them, so that it will enable them to have a profound knowledge of this dark period of our history and thus prevent it from ever occuring again.

Elvira Cuervo de Jaramillo
Director
Museo Nacional de Colombia (National Museum of Colombia)

Testimonies of barbarism

Santiago Londoño Vélez

"Colombia hurts me terribly"

FERNANDO BOTERO[1]

Distanced from the influence of the 20th century vanguards, a small number of contemporary figurative artists, possessors of an independent spirit, have managed to create authentic personal visions of the world that are nourished by the great tradition of classical painting and the freedoms won by the modern movements. Among them, the Colombian artist Fernando Botero (1932) plays a leading role. Following half a century of artistic work centered on an exaltation of the sensuality of the form, he found that he had to leave a testimony of the barbarism of Colombia. According to the artist:

> I was against that art which becomes a witness to its times in order to serve as a weapon. But in view of the magnitude of the drama that Colombia is going through, there came a moment when I felt a moral obligation to leave a testimony about an irrational period of our history.[2]

Contrary to what might be thought, this aim is not entirely novel to his work. The root of what is today a moving position on the Colombian tragedy is found in youthful experiences which, at the height of the period when he was training himself to be an artist, led him to an aesthetic of mourning. This is particularly evident in certain works with a marked symbolic power, as is the case with the watercolor *Mujer Llorando* (Weeping Woman, 1949). While it reveals a precocious interest in the expansion of volume and monumentality, in expressive terms it gives importance to a sensitive gaze that shares the suffering of the other.

During his youthful time on the Atlantic coast, Botero, under the influence of the ideals of Gauguin and the blue and pink period of Picasso, depicted episodes of the violence that scourged the country at that time in apprentice pieces like the one entitled *Frente al mar* (Facing the sea, 1952, awarded second prize at the IX Annual Salon of

Colombian Artists). It was inspired by a real event which he witnessed on the beaches of Tolú: two men drag their victim along, his hands and feet tied to a pole.

At the end of the 1950's, the terrible crimes committed in Bogotá by Nepomuceno Matallana became part of popular mythology with the novelistic reporting given to them by the Colombian media. Basing himself on the stories about this sinister personage, Botero painted several pictures which employed the lengthened format of the Renaissance predellas. Works like *Teresita la descuartizada* (Teresita, the woman cut into pieces, 1963), *Las noches del doctor Mata* (The nights of Doctor Kill, 1963) and *El asesinato de Ana Rosa Calderón* (The Murder of Ana Rosa Calderón, 1969) show a clear narrative intention, in which Colombian popular imagery, inflamed by the bloody incidents, is integrated with pictorial elements characteristic of European art, such as the format, color and composition. In this way Botero showed that, regardless of its origin, the anecdote may have a high artistic value, as had already become evident in his use of a sports hero for the picture *Apoteosis de Ramón Hoyos Vallejo* (1959).

Richly painted with a predominance of violet, *Obispos muertos* (Dead bishops, 1958), found in the collection of the National Museum of Colombia, is a large-format oil which may be interpreted as a metaphor for the violence of the mid-20th century, in which certain sectors of the clergy openly took a side in political matters. Sunk in an eternal sleep with their angular tiaras, the rounded prelates, arrayed in a massive accumulation, form a solid harmony of spheres which efficiently integrates form and color, a matter which becomes one of the aesthetic concerns of the artist.

In 1974, the loss of his son Pedrito led him to develop, with a particular intensity and within a style that was already fully consolidated, a refined artistic express of personal mourning. Staying faithful to his credo of the exaltation of tactile values, he created a kind of pictorial elegy in which he tries to recover the boy's image. He is displayed in different situations, the common denominator of which is the desire to eternalize him by means of a delicate poetic transposition in which color plays a fundamental role. Over and over again the innocent gaze of the child sinks into the void, accompanied by some of his toys seen in homey spaces that are converted into a kind of celestial scenario.

From there to the end of the 1980's, Botero occasionally dealt with subjects related to the violence in Co-

---

[1] *"I paint Colombia because it hurts me." Revista Diners*, Bogotá, February, 2000, pag. 20.

[2] Quoted in: Wilson Arcila, "Botero, con dolor de patria" (Botero: a patriotic sorrow), *Revista Diners,* Bogotá, March 2001, pag. 24.

lombia, as is the case with *La guerra* (The war, 1973), an ambitious tragicomic version that condenses the conflicts that were unleashed from 1948 onwards. It shows a vast and prolix hemispherical arrangement of the dead of diverse conditions, clinging to their weapons, investitures and banners. Among the paintings that anticipate the more extensive approach to the theme that he would undertake from 1997 onwards are *Cazador or guerrillero* (Hunter-guerrilla soldier, 1988), and particularly *La guerrilla de Eliseo Velázquez* (The Eliseo Velázquez guerrilla band), of the same year. This canvas stands out by virtue of its elaborate composition and harmonious palette, the means by which he manages to transform the dangerous members of an insurgent band into seemingly harmless individuals.

With *Masacre de Mejor Esquina* (The Massacre at Mejor Esquina, 1997), which was inspired by the murder of 28 people who were participating in a popular fiesta on March 4, 1988 in a rural district of the Department of Córdoba, the new slant of the artist's work is definitively initiated. In this stage real incidents that are not witnessed at first hand but known from the news awaken the need to shape a testimony to the violence of contemporary Colombia. As he stated,

> The artistic reconstruction of the conflict, which is finally reduced to a number of images or symbols, corresponds to the need one feels to not turn your back on the situation. My country has two faces. Colombia is that friendly world that I always paint, but it has also that terrible face of violence. Thus, at a certain moment, I have to show the other face of Colombia.[3]

In this work, as in the others that make up the series donated to the National Museum, it is not a matter of offering a journalistic illustration or an historical recreation but, rather, of producing a free artistic interpretation, as is shown by the fact that it was painted nine years after the event, there are only twelve personages in it and the sense of perspective is deliberately altered. The painter does not set out to change reality or illustrate a deed, but tries to capture and show constituent elements of the recent history of the country, so that both today and in the future it may serve as a reminder, or *memento mori*:

I don´t expect that these pictures are going to solve anything, because I know very well that art does not change anything. Those who are responsible for changes are the politicians. I only aim to leave the testimony of an artist who lived and felt his country and his time. It as though I were saying: "look at the madness we are living in, so that it does not happen again." I am not doing *l'art engagé*, that art which wishes to change things, because I don´t believe in that.[4]

Since then this gallery of the disasters of war caused by the sleep of reason, as it might be termed, paraphrasing Goya, has been increasing. It is made up of the victims and their killers, the same that are now called, with bureaucratic coldness, "the agents of the armed conflict." Both sides are painted and drawn with the same formal distance that envelops the typical personages and objects of Botero, but with an undisguised sentiment of pity for the afflicted and their tribulations. That wish which Botero has expressed to always paint as though he were painting fruit is present when he comes to construct the spaces and proportions. But the ominous content and the crudeness of the images introduce into his work for the first time a hitherto unseen sense of tragedy, in which the joy of living disappears and is replaced by a pained conscience. This rending is static and at times recalls the crucifixion scenes painted by Mantegna and Piero della Francesca. Everything is dominated by a sorrowful silence and a religious suffering marked by a patience and abnegation which not even the bursts of bullets, individually frozen in space, manage to interrupt as they go about their mortal work.

Una madre (A Mother, 1999), shows a mother bathed in tears before the coffin of her child, raising her arms in a gesture of powerlessness in a room in shadows. Another kneels in desolation before the open coffin, and still another, which is a skeleton with a vulture on her shoulder, holds her baby, reduced to bones in her lap, in *Madre e hijo* (Mother and child, 2000). Different versions, painted and drawn, of a weeping mother bring the above-mentioned youthful watercolor of 1949 up to date, marking an iconographic continuity in the work of Botero.

In *El desfile* (The procession, 2000), a veritable river of coffins in a collective burial, led by a bishop with a lighted

---

3 *Ibid.*

4 *Ibid.*

candle, descends in a march along the edge of a yellow-ocher town which has been mercilessly destroyed, while a bird of ill omen crosses the scene. The homes of the poor, savagely burnt down, are the backdrop of a bloody scene in *Masacre en Colombia* (2000), crossed by a wall that stretches out in perspective. Death is the last hope of prisoners and the tortured, as in *Un consuelo* (a consolation, 2000), or in several untitled works. In the face of these figures, it is worth recalling the artist's words:

> I reject realism, in the sense of copying reality. What I do is to construct a composition that conserves a decorative dimension even in dramatic situations, because a true painter can transform a tragic form like death into a decorative element.[5]

A distressing allegory of the triumph of death, which belongs to the tradition of this genre in European painting and at the same time goes back to José Guadalupe Posada, is *Viva la muerte* (Long live death, 2001). In the midst of a gloomy room full of coffins, the dominating figure of death rests as it contemplate the fruits of its annihilation; in the background a half-open door may represent the passage to the beyond. The sinister, extended skeleton bears the presidential sash on its breast, with the colors of the Colombian flag reversed, which may be a symbol of the new power which seems to rule the country instead of the civil authority.

At dawn on November 22, 2000, a group of sixty paramilitaries murdered at least forty-two people in the rural districts of Buenavista and Nueva Venecia, in the Ciéanaga Grande de Santa Marta marsh in the Department of Magdalena, while another thirty disappeared and nearly three thousand were displaced.[6] In Botero's version of these terrible events, entitled *Masacre de Ciénaga Grande* (2001), a single canoe is turned into the ship of death, guided by an invisible Charon. It majestically rides over the high seas of turbulent water, running into a broadside of bullets that ends the life of the seven fishermen who are in it. The fishing nets of the poor men hang over the edge of the boat as mute witnesses to the slaughter.

Masacre en la catedral (2002) is based on the killing that occurred in Bojayá, a settlement in the Department of the Chocó located near the river Atrato. The incident in which one hundred and eighteen people lost their lives, among them many children, occurred on May 2, 2002. The victims had sought refuge in the church of the village, which was destroyed without a second thought by the guerrilla during a battle with paramilitary groups. Botero heard the news on the radio and created a large-format picture, setting himself to "… encounter an aesthetic composition even in the midst of such drama. A true painter can transform something tragic, like death, into an aesthetic event."[7] The vertical image shows an instant inside the church during the trance of destruction; in the central axis the deathly-white skeletal figure of death is an exterminating angel which brandishes its fateful sword. Pieces of masonry, glass, wood and roof tiles fall to the ground, the roof caves in and the columns buckle. A number of corpses lie on the floor in a pile of rubble; on a wall to the right, the statue of a saint totters, while in the background a colonial alter, outside of time and space, is on the point of succumbing to the collapse.

Time and again, Botero's testimony is complemented by disfigured corpses, black vultures that hover over their remains or fly about like deadly signals, drowned bodies floating in the river, mothers and widows that disconsolately weep, displaced people without a future, thick skeletons, unpunished murderers, car bombs in the exact moment of explosion and even the devastating earthquake that occurred in Popayán in 1983, because not even Mother Nature has left the country in peace but only aggravated its sorrows. Only the beauty of the colors – applied at times with urgency, without the patient delight found in many of his paintings – and the harmony of the forms in these surprising compositions barely attenuate the cataclysm which they depict.

In the words of Botero,

> The feeling I had when I painted these pictures is not the same pleasure I feel when I am normally painting the world I paint. It is another sensation. The very fact of setting out, as an artist, to find a symbolic image

[5]   Botero, quoted by Pamela Biénzobas, in "Botero, testigo del dolor colombiano" (Botero: witness to the sorrow of Colombia), *Cosas*, N°. 284, Lima, January 2004.

[6]   www.monde-diplomatique.fr/cuaderno/plancolombia/derechoshumanos2001

[7]   "Y sigue tan campante" (As lively as ever), *Semana*, Bogotá, November 24, 2003.

that reflects the great drama of Colombia signifies a mental state that is not pleasant but painful.[8]

In the drawings and paintings new plastic elements emerge, which not only serve to introduce chromatic areas that balance or lend surprise to the composition or make it dynamic, but also turn into a whole new vocabulary in action which did not exist before in the iconography of the Colombian artist. Bodies drilled by bullets, coffins, machete wounds, spilled blood, grotesque skeletons, vultures that play a symbolic role, threads of blood, enormous firearms, reddened eyes, wasted rostrums, emotive gestures, flames of yellow cadmium, pieces of cars and buildings that fly through the air, people bound and blindfolded, blood-soaked knives and demolished houses – they form part of a hecatomb that threatens to be endless.

His palette, of vibrant colors in some cases and somber, muted ones in others, is fundamental to the attainment of the final atmosphere that envelops the paintings and helps to create a dynamic relationship between the spectator and the forms. The lively colors do not give a feeling of gaiety, since, considering the gravity of the deeds, they function, instead, to accentuate their unreal character: stunned, we witness the murder of a widow with her two children in front of a pink cathedral beneath a sweet cerulean-blue sky. The displaced family, completely bewildered, tries to survive with its belongings still bundled up, beneath a tent that is unexpectedly magenta. The chemical violet of a mother's dress shows a body wracked by sorrow and an electric-blue car, which resembles a toy, frames a kidnapping.

The neutral colors, achieved through lead grays, ochers, sepias, *verdaccios* (green underpainting) and some violet or blue shadows, define the atmosphere and establish a correspondence with the mournful symbolism, as happens in *Muerte* (Death, 2002), *Secuestrado* (Kidnapping victim, 2002), *Quiebrapatas* (Anti-personnel mine 2002) and *Desplazado* (Displaced person, 2002).

In the drawings, it as though the line wishes to mark a parenthesis in the virtuosity which has linked Botero to Ingres. It as though a hidden desperation or a lump in the throat were guiding and pressuring the hand that envelops the forms through the use of a graphite or sanguine pencil. It is pre-cisely in these drawing where one is able to see, with greater emphasis, the facial and corporeal expression of the emotional states of violence and its consequences. Decomposed rostrums, reddened eyes, twitching or entwined hands, prostrated bodies and pleading postures are found in *Grito* (Cry, 2002), *Tristeza* (Sorrow, 2002), *Sin esperanza* (Without hope, 2003), *Agonía* (Agony, 2002), *Ruego* (Plea, 2003), *De rodillas* (Kneeling, 2003).

Different horrible incidents are recorded in pieces like *Motosierra* (Chainsaw, 2003), *Un secuestro* (A kidnapping, 2003) – which hypothetically takes place in front of the former family home of the artist in Medellín, identified by the street number, 54-27 calle Mon y Velarde –, *Un crimen* (A crime, 2002) and *Sin compasión* (Without compassion, 2002). Imaginary portraits of those who carry out the barbaric deeds, whose features are given a characteristic rictus, produce a startling effects in drawing like *Verdugo* (Executioner, 2002), *Hombre armado* (Armed man, 2002) and *Sicario* (Hired killer, 2002).

The nature of the testimony that Botero leaves for present and future generations goes beyond a purely artistic or formal aim. His ideal of the art that helps us to escape the cruelty of life by offering a refuge of serenity and beauty is thoroughly transformed. While he does not let himself go like an expressionist dominated by his own feelings about such disasters, neither does he turn the suffering that endlessly flow through these images into pornography. With a restrained indignation, he allows the different incidents with their anonymous protagonists to march across the canvas and paper, some frozen in the very instant of the individual or collective tragedy, others caught in an intimate moment of weeping or unbearable pain.

These images are not a summons to rebellion or social protest: they have no ideological affiliation or relation to a political movement, and are free of a moralizing sermon or even a voice of hope. For that very reason they are not an engaged art, in the conventional sense of the term. The commitment continues to be with art itself, it is worth noting; with the expressive needs of the creative artist and his own laws. It is a matter, then, of a compassionate gaze, exacerbated and full of solidarity, which is furnished with the highest ethical and aesthetic sense—a gaze which offers a personal testimony that not even the most indifferent person may ignore, whose aim is to make it impossible to forget so many lives cut down by barbarism.

[8]   Arcila, *op. cit.*

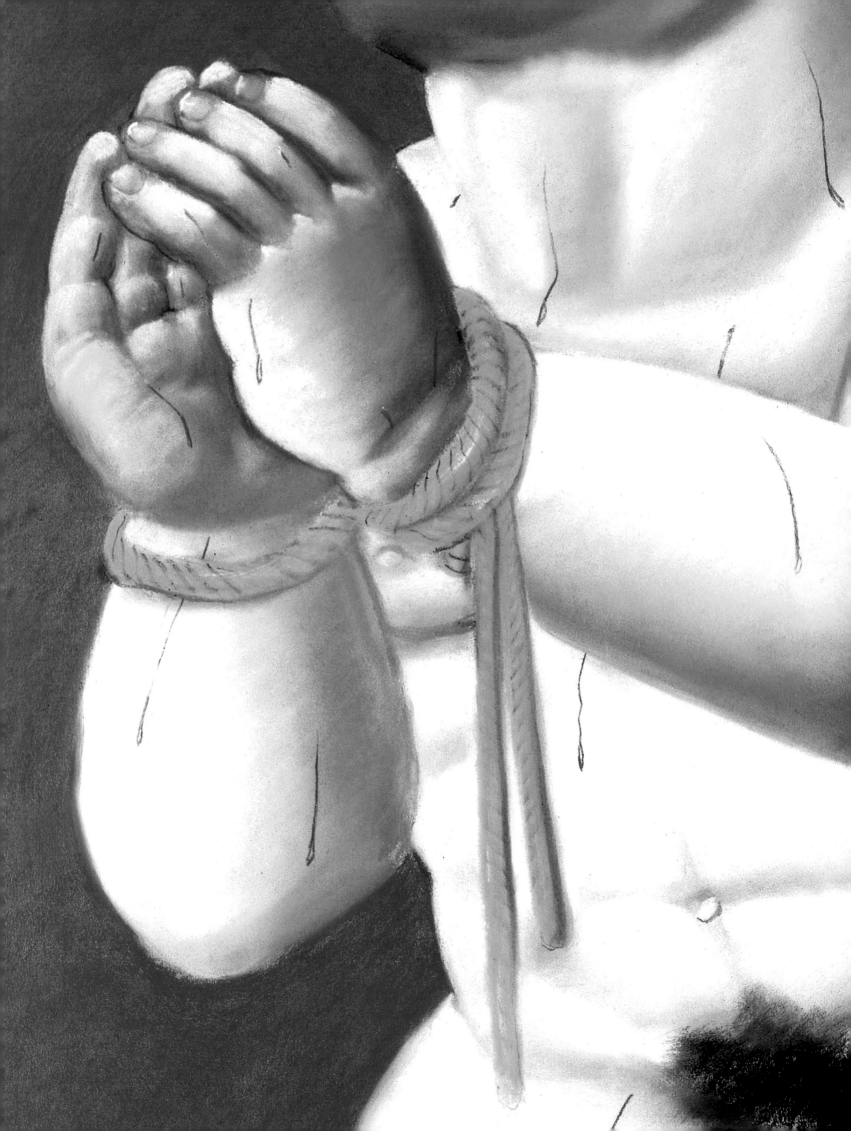

Weeping woman
(Mujer llorando)
1999
Oil on canvas
36 x 29 cm

"My country has two faces. Colombia is that friendly world that I always paint, but it also has that terrible face of violence. Thus, at a certain moment, I have to show the other face of Colombia."

FERNANDO BOTERO

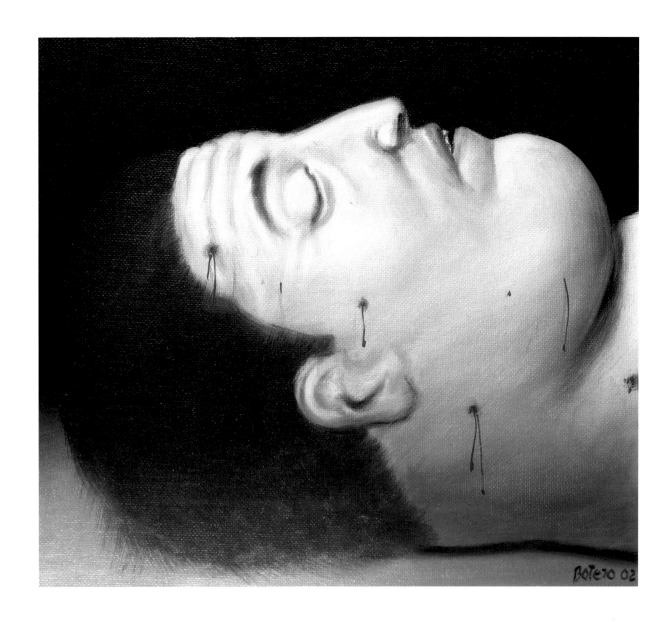

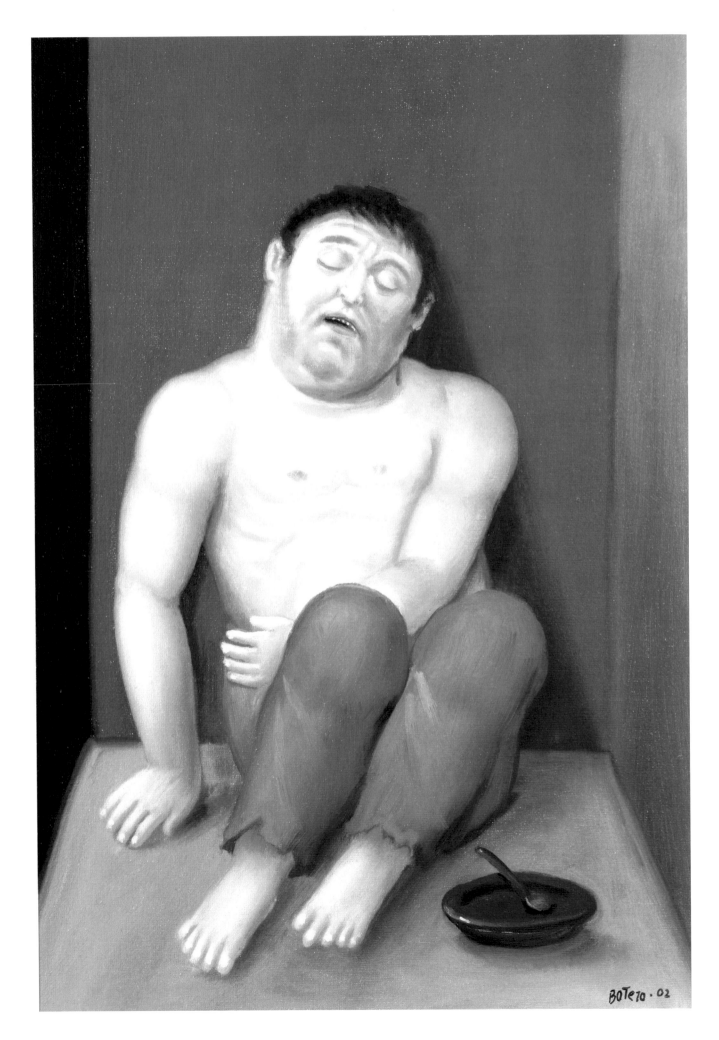

Kidnapping victim
(Secuestrado)
2002
Oil on canvas
59 x 49 cm

Agony
(Agonía)
2002
Pastel
98 x 72 cm

Untitled
1999
Oil on canvas
38 x 32 cm

A consolation
(Un consuelo)
2000
Oil on canvas
33 x 41 cm

Mother and child
(Madre e hijo)
2000
Oil on canvas
31 x 39 cm

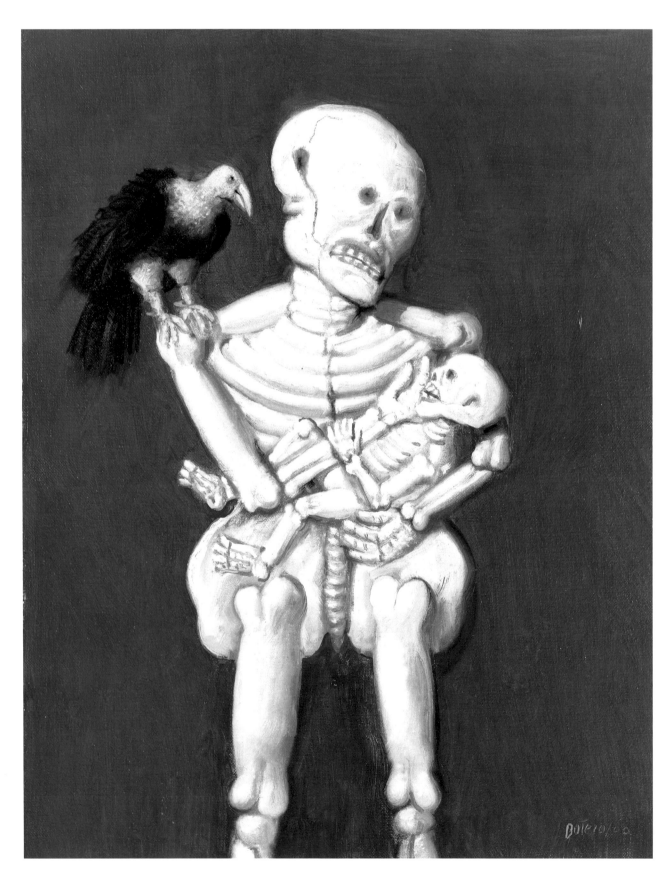

Untitled
1999
Oil on canvas
26 x 34 cm

Mother
(Una madre)
2001
Oil on canvas
37 x 45 cm

Mother
(Una madre)
1999
Oil on canvas
38 x 32 cm

River Cauca
(Río Cauca)
2002
Oil on canvas
48 x 67 cm

Below,
Long Live Death!
(Viva la muerte)
2001
Oil on canvas
44 x 33 cm

Opposite page,
Death in the Cathedral
(La muerte en la catedral)
2002
Oil on canvas
196 x 131 cm

Page 32,
Anti-personnel mine
(Quiebrapatas)
2002
Oil on canvas
56 x 44 cm

Page 33,
Displaced person
(Desplazado)
2002
Oil on canvas
61 x 44 cm

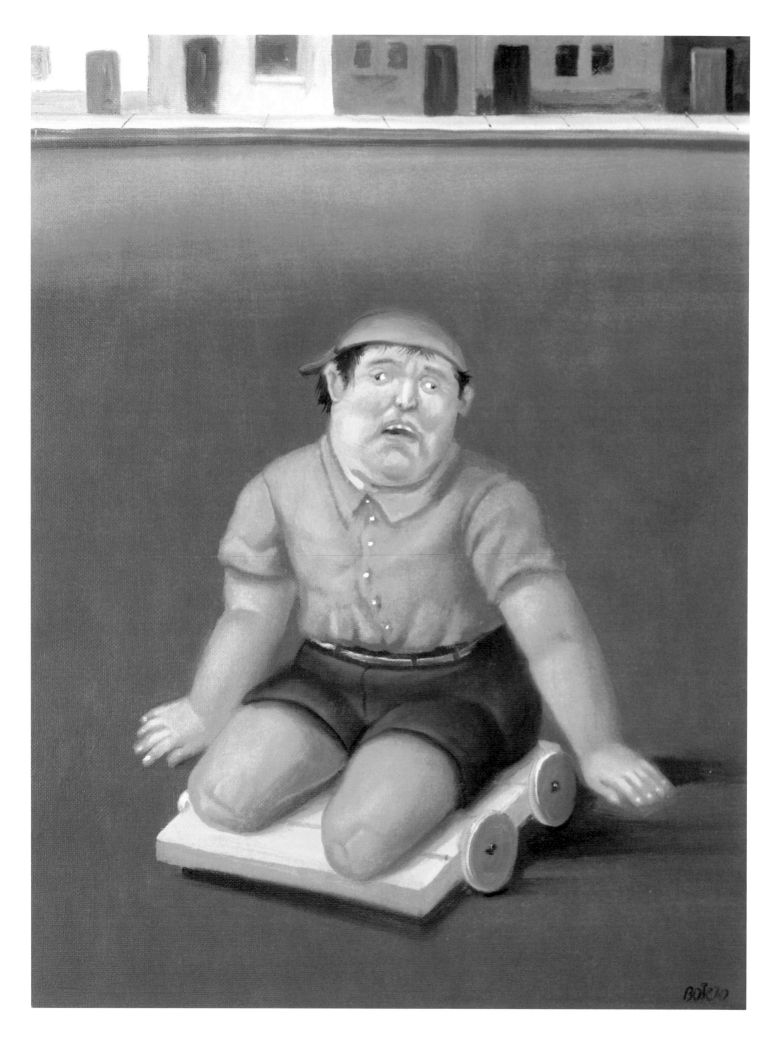

Massacre in the Ciénaga Grande
(Masacre de Ciénaga Grande)
2001
Oil on canvas
157 x 200 cm

Hunter
(El cazador)
1999
Oil on canvas
39 x 27 cm

Car bomb
(Carro bomba)
1999
Oil on canvas
28 x 33 cm

Kidnapping
(Un secuestro)
2002
Oil on canvas
78 x 95 cm

**Kidnapping victim
(Secuestrada)**
2002
Oil on canvas
51 x 37 cm

Pages 40-41,
**Massacre in Colombia
(Masacre en Colombia)**
2000
Oil on canvas
129 x 192 cm

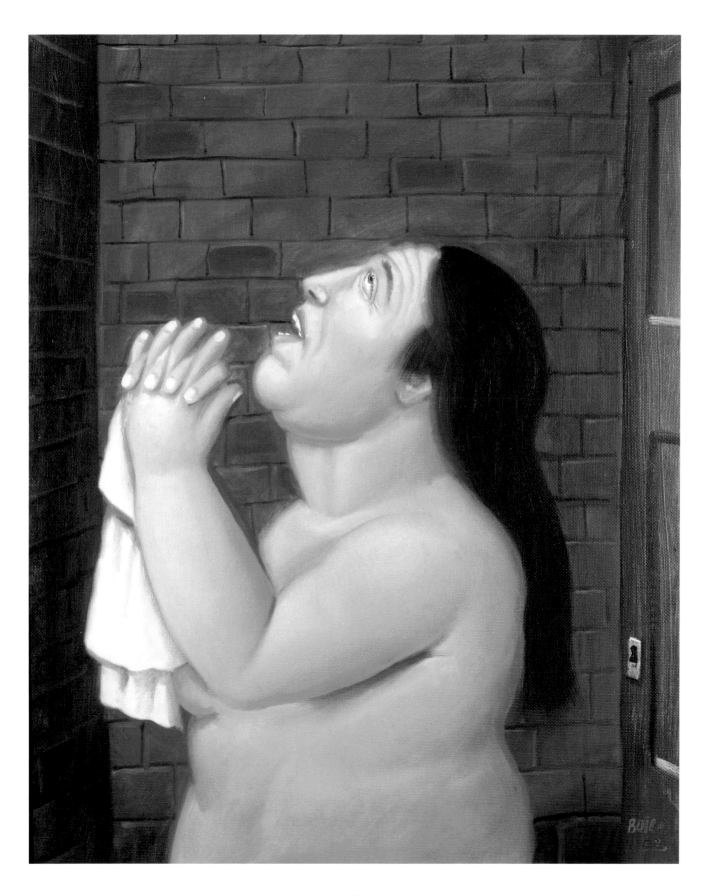

41

Slaughter of the innocents
(Matanza de los inocentes)
1999
Oil on canvas
45 x 32 cm

Massacre
(Masacre)
2000
Oil on canvas
40 x 32 cm

" I must point out that the feeling I had when I painted these pictures is not
the same pleasure I feel when I am normally painting the world I paint. It is
another sensation. The very fact of setting out, as an artist, to find a symbolic
image that reflects the great drama of Colombia signifies a mental state that
is not pleasant but painful. The artistic reconstruction of the conflict, which is
finally reduced to a number of images or symbols, corresponds to the need
one feels to not turn your back on the situation."

FERNANDO BOTERO

Sorrow
(Tristeza)
2002
Pencil, ink
19 x 17 cm

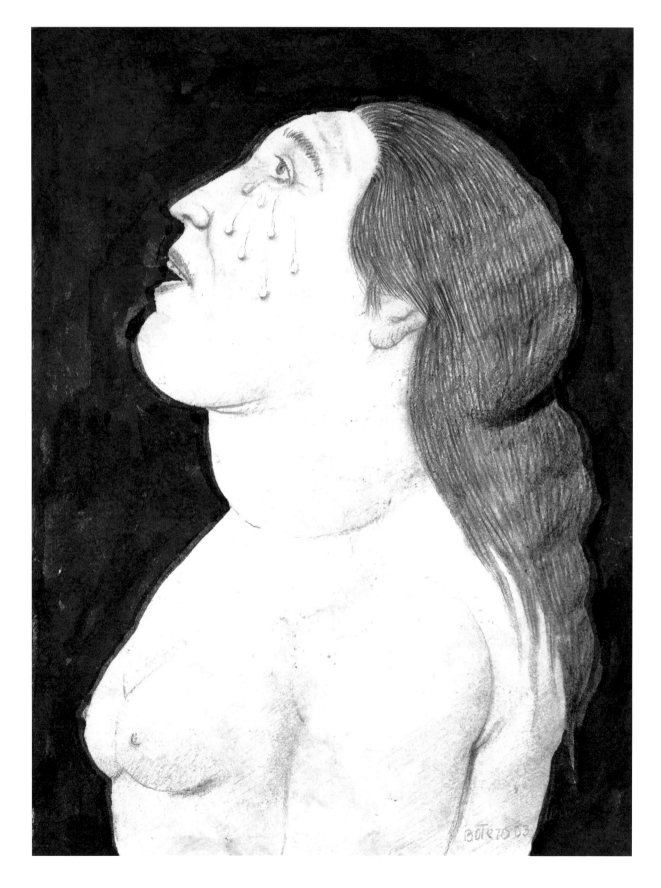

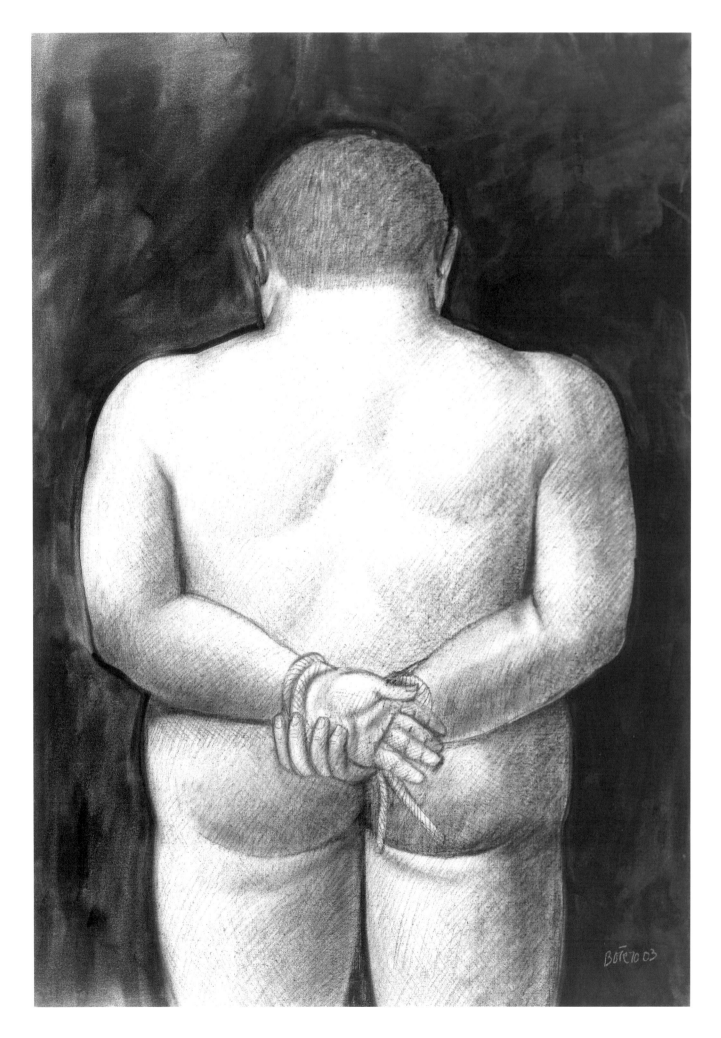

Chainsaw
(Motosierra)
2003
Pencil, ink
15 x 19 cm

A crime
(Un crimen)
2002
Pencil
31 x 41 cm

**Weeping woman
(Mujer llorando)**
2002
Pencil
39 x 30 cm

"These pictures are a way of rejecting violence. I am the person who least supports solving things through force and brutality. Conflicts are resolved with dialogues, concessions, understanding. Violence is a cancer, a great cancer that struck the country and I am against violent acts as a solution."

FERNANDO BOTERO

Plea
(Ruego)
2003
Pencil
40 x 30 cm

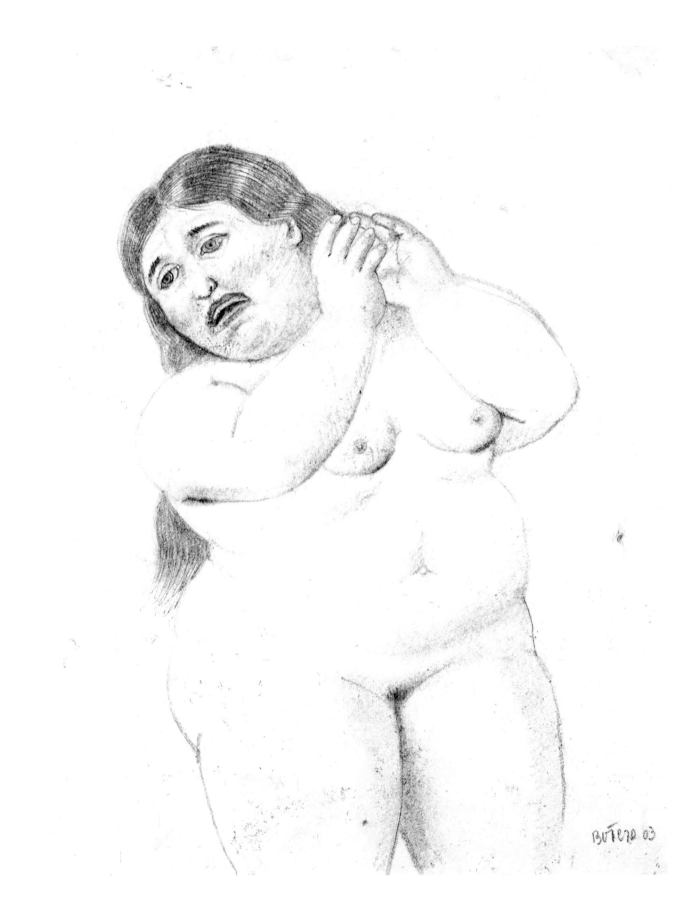

Kneeling
(De rodillas)
2003
Pencil
37 x 30 cm

Botero 03

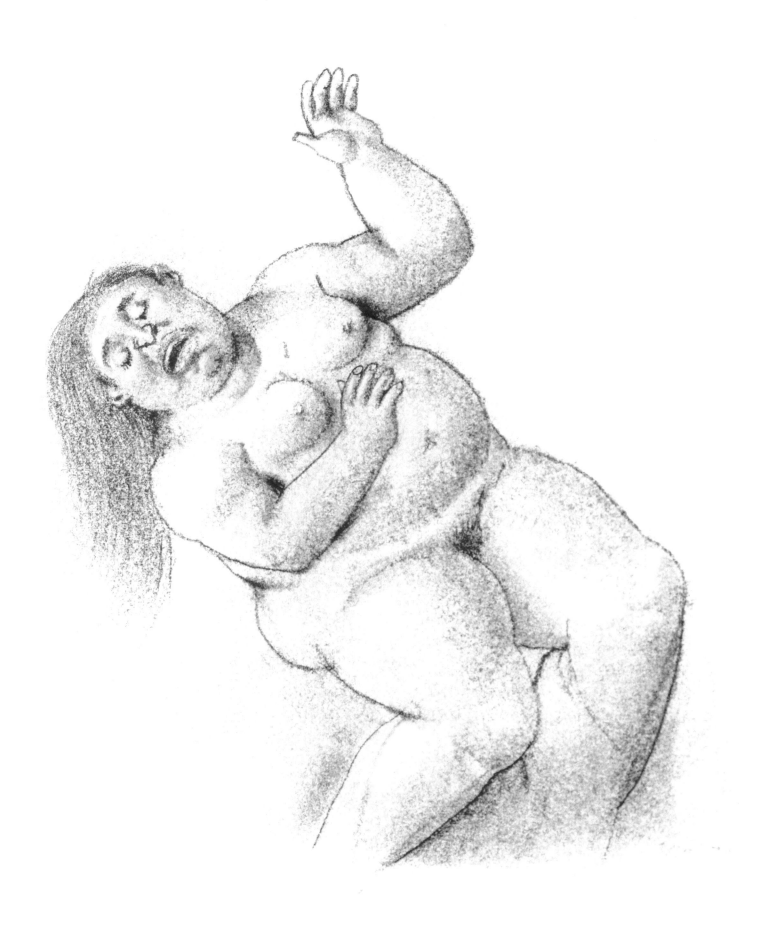

Cry
(Grito)
2002
Pencil
18 x 15 cm

Defeated
(Vencida)
2002
Pencil
24 x 18 cm

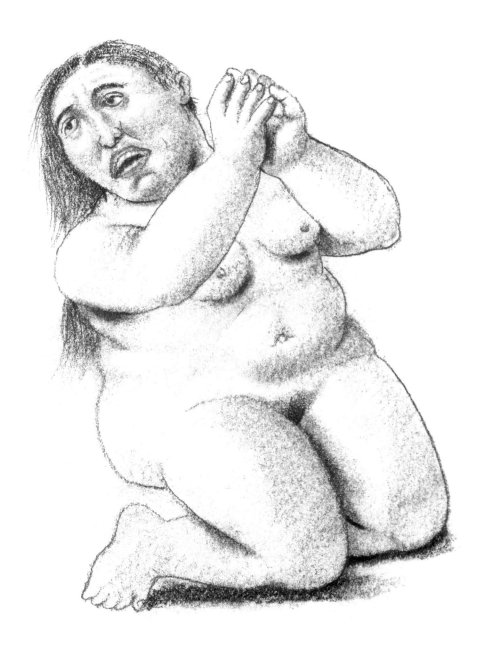

Botero 02

" I was against that art which becomes a witness to its times in order to serve as a weapon. But in view of the magnitude of the drama that Colombia is going through, there came a moment when I felt a moral obligation to leave a testimony about an irrational period of our history..."

FERNANDO BOTERO

Below,
Another crime
(Otro crimen)
2002
Sanguine
20 x 27 cm

Page 60,
Executioner
(Verdugo)
2002
Pencil
39 x 29 cm

Page 61,
Armed man
(Hombre armado)
2002
Pencil
28 x 20 cm

61

Untitled
2003
Pencil
38 x 30 cm

Without compassion
(Sin compasión)
2002
Pencil
27 x 20 cm

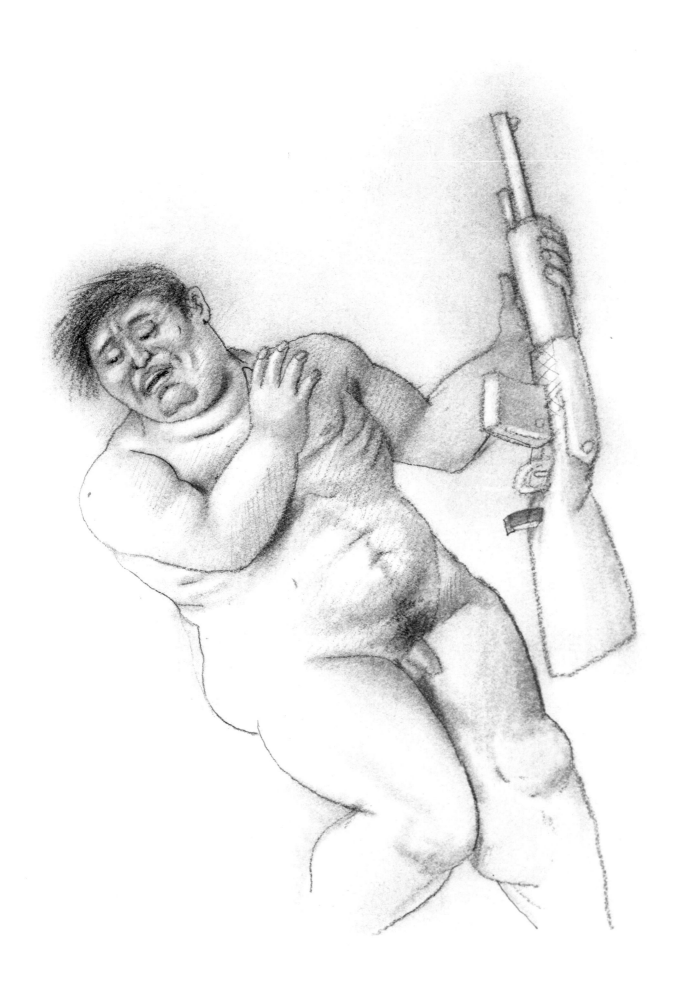

Death
(Muerte)
2002
Pencil
41 x 31 cm

Falling man
(Hombre cayendo)
2002
Pencil
41 x 31 cm

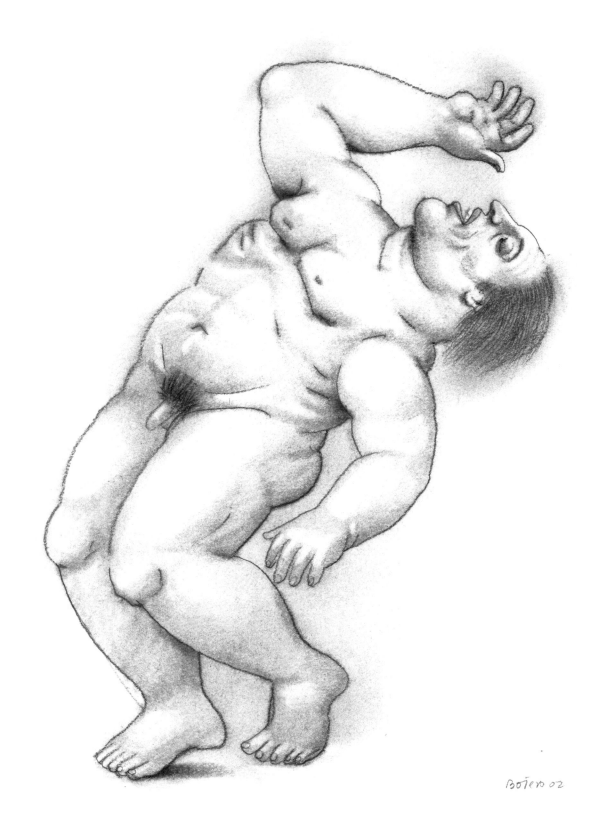

Botero 02

" I only aim to leave the testimony of an artist who lived and felt his country and his time. It as though I were saying: "look at the madness we are living in, so that it does not happen again." I am not doing engaged art, that art which wishes to change things, because I don't believe in that."

FERNANDO BOTERO

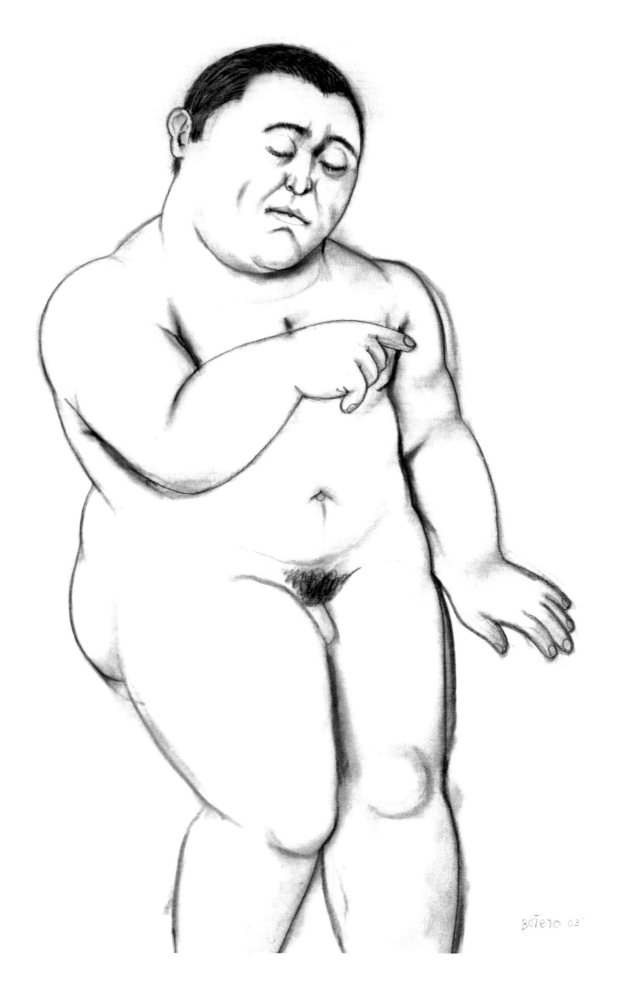

BOTERO 03

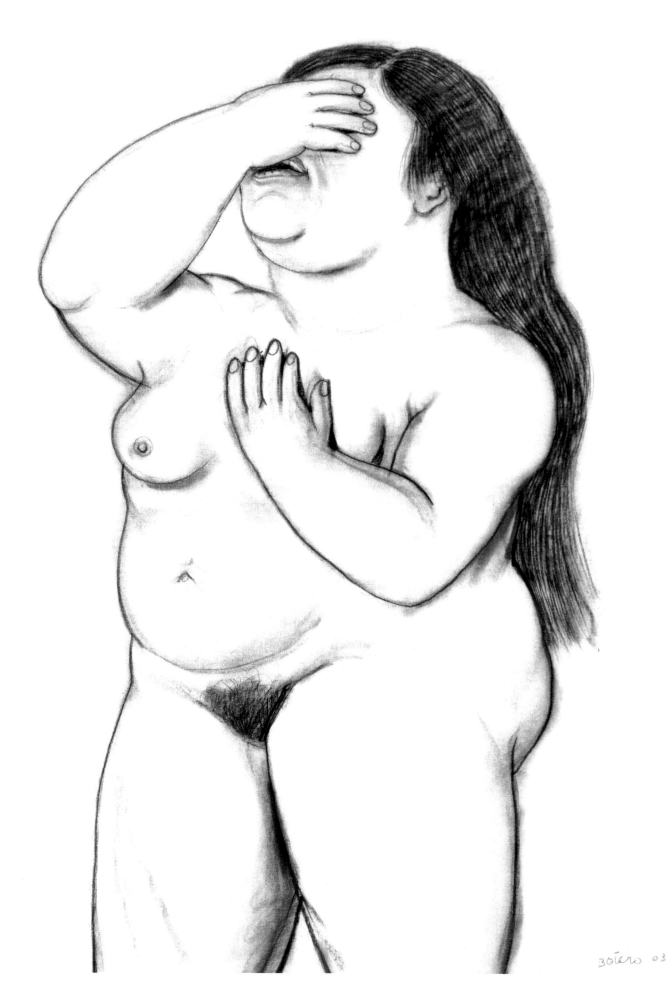

**Displaced people
(Desplazados)**
2004
Watercolor
31 x 40 cm

**Displaced people
(Desplazados)**
2004
Pencil
40 x 31 cm

The Fernando Botero Collection of the National Museum of Colombia

Beatriz González

History of the collection

"The best way to understand Botero is to see the National Museum of Colombia," wrote the eminent Italian critic Vittorio Sgarvi when he visited the country in 1991.[1] Thirteen years have passed since he wrote those words and during the last decade of the 20th century the collections of the painter from the Department of Antioquia have been the subject of extraordinary happenings. Botero became a great patron of art for institutions like the Luis Ángel Arango Library in Bogotá, to which he donated, in 1998, 80 works of 19th and 20th century Western art from his private collection and 125 of his own creations. As a mark of gratitude, the Banco de la República (the Central Bank) created the Botero Museum.

The other institution that benefited from his generosity was the Museum of Antioquia, to which he gave, in the year 2000, twenty-one works of contemporary art from his private collection and 85 of his own works, thus complementing two previous donations: the first in 1976, for the creation of the Pedro Botero Hall – in honor of his youngest son, who tragically died in Spain in 1974 – which was made up 16 paintings and pastels; and the second in 1984, to create a Sculpture Gallery. Thanks to his support, in the year 2000 the Museum of Antioquia was transformed into a cultural center which "turns it into a field for a living reflection on our reality."[2]

The National Museum of Colombia was the first beneficiary of his generosity, at a time when the painter was still unknown outside of Colombia. In October 1960, he decided to donate his work *Lección de guitarra* (Guitar Lesson, 1960) to that museum. The director at that time was the museum expert and artist Teresa Cuervo, whose sensitivity enabled her to foresee the future renown of Botero, so that she hung the painting in the Rotunda of the museum, alongside the works of great Colombian painters like Andrés de Santa María (1860-1945). At that time Botero was the center of heated polemics and his passionate defender was the noted critic Marta Traba. The question that comes to mind is why he decided to donate that work to such a traditional museum, one that was associated

with the "Establishment" and was the scenario of the official salons of art? The answer is very simple: in the first place it was the only museum in the Colombian capital at that time and Botero has always worshipped museums, especially those with a great tradition, like El Prado, the Louvre and the Ufizzi.

Ever since he was a young man his ambition was to exhibit his work in such museums. He was certain that the work he donated, the *Lección de guitarra*, was a "museum piece." His other reason was a practical one. In that era he had taken the decision to settle in the United States and it was better, he thought, to put his pictures in a safe place. The proof of it is that he left a group of paintings in the museum which, years later, he sent for, among them *La apoteosis de Ramón Hoyos Vallejo* (The apotheosis of Ramón Hoyos Vallejo, 1959). Only one of these paintings which he left behind, *Arzodiabolomaquia* (Archdiabolimachy, 1960), now forms part of the collection of the National Museum. In 1976, while the building was being remodelled under the direction of Emma Araújo de Vallejo, this painting, was discovered, rolled up, in a corner of the auditorium. Years later, in 1998, the artist donated it to the institution.

A work of his early years, *Contrapunto* (Counterpoint, 1957) reached the National Museum by the official route. In the X Annual Salon of Colombian Artists, this painting was awarded the second prize, which was shared with works by Alejandro Obregón (1920-1992) and Jorge Elías Triana (1921-1999). The prize consisted of a "Silver medal and diploma." This important event had been suspended for five years and its reinitiation was one of the symbols of the end of the military dictatorship of General Gustavo Rojas Pinilla, who had become President through a coup d´état.

We do not know for certain whether the Cultural Extension Office of the Ministry of Education had held onto both the work for which Botero received the prize and the one that received the first prize, Lucy Tejada´s (born 1924) *Mujeres sin hacer nada* (Idle Women), which was shared by the painting *Elementos para un eclipse* (Elements for an eclipse), by Enrique Grau (b. 1920). One possible explanation is that a regulation that "a subsequent commission will choose those works which, in their judgement, deserve to be acquired for the Museum of Modern Art" may have played a role.[3]

The dynamic art critic Marta Traba, who was determined to refound the Museum of Modern Art, an institution that had

---

[1] Sgarvi, Vittorio. "Consagración en Florencia. El nuevo mundo de Botero" (Consecration in Florence: the new world of Botero), Lecturas Dominicales, *El Tiempo*, 28 July 1991, pag. 8.

[2] Fernández, Carlos Arturo. "El Medellín de Botero. Un universo de sentido" (Botero´s Medellín: a universe of meaning), *Donación Botero Museo de Antioquia*. Bogotá, Villegas Editores, 2000, pag. 26.

[3] AA. VV. *50 Años Salón Nacional de Artistas* (50 Years of the National Salon of Artists), Bogotá, Colcultura, 1990, pag. 316.

not been given official recognition by the Ministry of Education, was probably a member of that commission and thus, the Cultural Extension Office, when it realized that the new museum was not an official one, held onto the works. Years later, that Office was transformed into Colcultura (The Colombian Institute of Culture), which sent the works to the National Museum in 1981.

On August 29, 1985 – twenty-five years after Botero's first donation in 1960 – he gave a second gift to the National Museum, which was accompanied by an explanatory letter. The letter stated that:

1. I make this donation to the Colombian people and the depository of the work is the National Museum.
2. Its custody and permanent maintenance are the responsibility of that institution, in the person of its director.
3. The work may not be removed from its site for loans of any kind, since I consider the National Museum to be the best place for it to be appreciated and divulged, because of the large public that visits that precinct.
4. The continuous movement of works of art is extremely harmful for their integrity.
5. Works of art suffer from changes in environment and light and from being transported, for which reason they should not be moved from their original site.
6. On being donated to the National Museum-Colcultura, the pictures of the artist Fernando Botero become part of the national heritage of Colombians and for that reason, must be cared for and preserved as objects that belong to the nation.
7. The works may not be reproduced for commercial purposes and must have the authorization of myself or my representative when they are reproduced for cultural purposes.

The 13 paintings and 2 watercolors represent some of the stages of his artistic development, although most of them are dated between 1980 and 1984. The 1950´s are represented by two works of singular importance, *Los obispos muertos* (The Dead Bishops, 1958) y *El niño de Vallecas* (after Velázquez's famous portrait of the court dwarf Francisco Lezcano, 1959).

While there are no works from the 1960´s, there are five from the following decade: *Pedro* (1971), *La naranja* (The orange, 1977*), El árbol* (The tree, 1979), *El bosque* (The forest, 1979) and *Los techos* (Roofs, 1979). The remaining works, which include two watercolors, were done between 1980 and 1984: *Silla con guitarra* (Chair with guitar, 1980), *Florero* (Flower vase, 1980), *La calle* (The street, 1980), *Naturaleza muerta* (Still life, 1983), *Mesa de cocina* (Kitchen table, 1983), *Colombiana* (Colombian woman, 1983), *La quebrada* (The stream, 1983), *20 de julio* (July 20th, 1984).

By virtue of its dedication to Colombian history, the National Museum of Colombia has been interested in completing the sequence of works which show the development of Botero's career. For that reason, in 1989 it decided to carry out an inventory of the artist's works that were found in public institutions. This enterprise led to the discovery of two interesting paintings in the Ministry of Education: one done in Tolú in 1952, *Sin título* (Untitled), and the other, *Mujeres peinándose* (Women doing their hair), done in 1953. Years later, in 1993, the Ministry agreed to transfer these works to the Museum's galleries.

In 1996, in a philanthropic gesture prompted by the director of the National Museum of Colombia, Elvira Cuervo de Jaramillo, the Banco Popular donated its collection to the National Museum of Colombia. Three paintings done by Botero in the 1950´s formed part of that donation: *La italiana* (Italian woman, 1954), a predella with the *Narrativa de la vida de un santo* (Narrative of the life of a saint, 1959) y *Los girasoles* (Sunflowers,1959). With the acquisition of these works, there was no doubt that the initial decade of the artist's career became well represented.

In the year 2003, the painter decided to donate 48 of his recent works to the National Museum. As he stated in an interview, because of their historic nature, these works should belong to that institution. With this latest donation the Museum's collection of his work has been brought up to date. It consists of 23 oils and 25 drawings that deal with the dramas of the current war in Colombia.

When you look at the collection from a curatorial standpoint, you reach the conclusion that the collection offers an exemplary coverage of the artist's career, except for his work of the 1960´s. Although it contains two notable works dating from the early part of that decade, worked in an open brushstroke and strong colors – *Lección de guitarra* and *Arzodiabolomaquia* – those paintings do not show the transition towards the closed brushstroke and tonal colors that characterized his style in the second half of the 1960´s, among which *La familia presidencial* (The Presidential family, 1967) stands out, which belongs to the New York Museum of Modern Art.

Analysis of the collection

We might ask ourselves why the Italian critic Sgarvi said that you had to go to the National Museum of Colombia to understand Botero. There are two answers. In the first place, the halls of the Museum that are devoted to the diversity of pre-Hispanic art exhibit a variety of ceramic pieces which art scholars consider to be closely related to the work of the painter from Antioquia. In addition, ever since its move in 1948 to the building which had served as the penitentiary of Cundinamarca – known as the Panopticon – the Museum has exhibited works like *Policarpa Salavarrieta marcha al suplicio* (ca.1825, a portrayal of the execution of one of the martyrs of the Colombian Independence movement), which the painter was able to study and, in a certain way, they were forerunners of his style by virtue of their charming and rounded ingenousness.

In the second place, in the gallery devoted to the "Early Moderns", the historic sequence of the development of the artist's work is displayed. Thus, if someone wants to know how the phenomenon of Botero arose, he will find the crucial stages of his work exhibited there, from its beginnings to the present time. In that space the visitor will not only find the chronological sequence, but the ten landmarks that make up his artistic career.

1. In search of identidy

His early talent was recognized by jurors and critics. He won his first triumphs in Bogotá at the age of 19. On the occasion of the Second Prize for Painting that was awarded to him in 1952 at the IX Salon of Colombian Artists, Eduardo Mendoza Varela wrote: "An excellent canvas, excellent without reservations … a valiant sense of color … his spontaneity, his strength."[4]

Color and strength are the characteristics of *Coco* (1951) and *Mujeres peinándose* (1953), the earliest works of Botero that are exhibited in the Museum, which represent his initial stage, when he was under the benign influence of Gauguin and Picasso. The Peruvian writer Vargas Llosa refers to the stage of his work in Tolú, "a village on the Caribbean coast," where "he spends a number of months – following the ex-

ample of Gauguin – devoted to painting the world of the natives and the seascapes."[5]

Another youthful work is *Contrapunto* (1957), which was honored with a prize in the X National Salon. Some of the characteristics of his painting are already present in it: the pink, blue, grey and green coloring; the strong volume hinted at by the brushstrokes and the planes of color. Although it is figurative, the work has an abstract structure. It is divided into four segments and each one reveals the influences he may have recevied, among those that of Alejandro Obregón. The critics enthusiastically commented on his chromatic sense:

> Fernando Botero's ambition to reach a complete mastery of color is more and more evident. His pictures have been following a path where the painter's aspiration, we believe, is the desire to attain a fully plastic language of color, one that will be able to contain a special poetic realism, of very loose expression, without impositions and with only the merest hints: a path, what is more, where his central concern lies in a virtuousity of unusual ranges of color.[6]

These unusual ranges intensified a year later, in his exhibition at the Biblioteca Nacional (National Library) with *Los girasoles* (1959), and the Mona Lisas which overflow with magenta and ultramarine-blue brushstrokes.

2. Religion

Religion, soldiers and the state are the three bulwarks behind which the life of the nation runs its course. Botero employs them as a subject that allows him to express his pictorial humor.

The roots of the religious theme, one of the most frequent in his work, are found in Colombia in general and in the Department of Antioquia in particular. Bishops appear in all the periods of his painting. They become the protagonists of varied adventures: they fly through the air as they are carried away by demons, *Arzodiabolomaquia* (1960); expel demons, *Narrativa de la vida de un santo* (1960); wander, lost, through sensual

4   Mendoza Varela, Eduardo. "La pintura en el IX Salón de Artistas" (Painting in the IX Salon of Artists), *El Espectador*, 9 August 1952.

5   Vargas Llosa, Mario. *Un latinoamericano entre los clásicos* (A Latin American among the classics). Bogotá, Galería el Museo, 1987.

6   Airó, Clemente. "En el Museo Nacional. El X Salón de Artistas Colombianos" (In the National Museum: The X Salon of Colombian Artists), *El Tiempo*, 26 September 1957.

Kitchen table (detail)
(Mesa de cocina)
1983
Oil on canvas
191 x 126 cm

jungles or narrow streets, as in *La calle* (1980); swim in the sea; voyage in boats and visit Rome. Popular traditions are present in the anecotes that he relates. *Los obispos muertos* (1958), begins a series at the end of the 1950's in which he places some of these figures on top of others, with their eyes closed and dressed in their vestments and crosiers, so that they resemble big still lifes of fruits. When a woman journalist asked him about the meaning of the bishops in his work, he replied, "I have nothing against the bishops, as some think ... What happens is that it is a fabulous subject matter and one that been kept intact since the Renaissance."[7] According to Marta Traba,

> the world needed more inhabitants and Botero invented the bishops. He took them from the true and invented lives of the saints. He laid them down with their absorbed and replete air, the splendorous mitre placed on the ground, as their dreams made the paradisiacal apples grow. He used them as the protagonists of epic entries into imaginary cities, where the rounded mass of the people roll beneath the hoofs of their cardboard horses. He piled them up in an implacable pyramid of mitres and heads and hands, irremediably asleep beneath their pompous ecclesiatical adornments.[8]

Recent studies have speculated that there is a political meaning in his work which has to do with the strong traditional power of the clergy in Antioquia.

> Botero's adolescence was marked by the assassination of the Liberal-party leader Jorge Eliécer Gaitán on April 9, 1948, which provoked riots that even led to the destruction of properties belonging to the Catholic Church. In June an Episcopal Conference was held to evaluate the evils which Communism and Liberalism had brought and it was decided to increase the number of parishes in the country ... When a political pact was made between the Liberals and Conservatives in 1958, the year in which this picture was painted, the electoral power of the Catholic Church disappeared.[9]

3. Reinterpretation of the history of art

A reinterpretation of the works of Leonardo, Piero della Francesca, Mantegna, Velázquez, Rubens and Cézanne, in particular, has been a constant in the work of the artist, who has declared that he does these pictures "only in order to learn from universal painting." Time and again, Botero returns to the masterpieces of European art, not with the aim of copying the great painters, but only to render homage to those who inspired him to work. However, he has always kept one eye on the Renaissance and the other on modern art. In his versions of *El niño de Vallecas* by Velázquez, he displays the creation of a pictorial figure of his own, based on the subject matter. He makes use of several kinds of brushstroke, some free and others tight, and a varied range of color that in some places responds to the volume and in others is independent of it.

Although he has expressed his dislike of abstract art and his lack of interest in U.S. painting, in the weft of free brushstrokes with which he works the arms and body of *El Niño de Vallecas* (1959) it is impossible not to feel the presence of a Pollock (1912-1956) or a De Kooning (1904-1997): "I did as many as ten or eleven versions of the boy in the course of a month," the artist remarks, "they were very sensual in the handling of color: perhaps there was an influence of the U.S. action painters."[10] In an interview in 1972, the painter stated:

> the first pictures that I exhibited in Colombia, in collective exhibitions around the 1940's, are surprisingly similar to the ones I currently paint. At that time I preferred to paint watercolors: scenes of marketplaces, in which fat people appeared amidst voluminous objects. In that epoch, art, even in reproductions, was almost totally unknown to me. Later I discovered the history of art and I copied everything: from caveman paintings to those of our times. In my second one-man show, which opened in Bogotá in 1952, there was such a variety of styles that people thought it was a collective one.[11]

[7] Valencia Diago, Gloria. "Estoy a favor de la anécdota y el arte impuro, dice Botero" (I am in favor of the anecdote and impure art, says Botero), *El Tiempo*, 1 March 1964.

[8] Traba, Marta. *Seis artistas contemporáneos* (Six contemporary artists). Bogotá, Alberto Barco Editores, 1963.

[9] Calderón Olaya, Marta. *Cartilla para elaborar contenidos de cuadros de colecciones permanentes en museos públicos* (Pamphlet on working out the contents of pictures in the permanent collections of public museums). Unpublished. 1996.

[10] AA. VV. *Fernando Botero*. Washington: Hirshhorn Museum, 1979.

[11] Von Bonin, Wibke. "Botero", *El Tiempo. Lecturas Dominicales*, Bogotá, 27 February 1972.

4. A mastery of his calling

Botero has treated color with great freedom from the very beginning. *Lección de guitarra* (1960) (Guitar Lesson) is the best example of his determination to transmute the conventional logic of painting. In the first place, he reverses the usual techniques, so that oil painting seems to have been worked in pastel. It has that quality given by the dust of the pigment on the surface of the canvas. The brushstrokes simulate chalk marks and seize hold of the range and the tones of pastels.

In the second place, he inverts the values and qualities of the forms. Skin may be silk or ceramics and ceramics and silk, skin. In the third place, by virtue of his mastery of his calling, he manages to make objects and figures which are weighty in real life fly and all that is light turn heavy. Figures of great volume fly through his pictures.

In the opinion of the art critic Marta Traba: "The passion for converting, contrasting and placing in evidence the expressive force of a world whose proportions exclusively depend on the sentiments which each form evokes in the artist gives Botero the opportunity to execute his best pictures."[12]

5. Drawing

From the beginning Botero has essentially been a draughtsman. His mastery of pencil, charcoal, ink, pastel and watercolor allow him to vary forms and surfaces and force the volumes to take over the surface of the picture. In this sense, he acts like an academic artist who, thanks to his knowledge of his calling, imposes his forms.

There is a strong tradition of watercolor in Antioquia, which may derive from the applied arts of its silverwork industry or the technical drawings used in mining and engineering. From the beginning of the twentieth century the artists of Antioquia showed a growing skill in that medium. The students of Pedro Nel Gómez (1898-1984), among whom Débora Arango (1905) stood out, worked in watercolors. Débora had a longing for large-format paper and to satisfy it, glued together sheets of standard size to obtain large surfaces. At the age of 16, while still an adolescent, Botero received instruction on how to "splash on" watercolors from his teacher Rafael

Sáenz (1910-1998). When he went to live in Europe he was able to work watercolors without limitations of size, thanks to the highly-developed paper industry there, which enabled him to order non-commercial formats. In *Florero* (1980) we can see his gusto for expanding the form by rapidly working the water and pigment on large surfaces.

6. The rounded

Marta Traba describes the process whereby the painter arrives at the rotund: "Botero goes on enlarging the figure until it comes to cover almost the whole of the picture and circulation becomes checked by that irrepressible and monstruous expansion. The canvas is drowned by the image."[13] However, in a nearly metaphysical reflection, it is the painter himself who becomes responsible for explaining his aim, when he affirms. "My basic interest is to paint an orange that is more of an orange, that will be all oranges, the abstract of all of them."[14]

In the course of time there have been diverse explanations for the origins of his quest for the rotund. The first of these is the prosaic one of the painter, who attributes it to chance: he remembers that he was painting a guitar and the circular hole (mouth) of the sounding box turned out too small and the guitar grew. This may be seen in the watercolor *Silla con guitarra* (1980) (Chair with guitar). However, there are other versions. When he was young, he used to visit the house of the painter from Antoquia Ignacio Gómez Jaramillo (1910 - 1970) in the evenings and there he discovered on a shelf some ceramic figures of great beauty made in the Colombian town of Ráquira, among them a horse with a jockey, the form of which moved him a great deal. It is also said that he was impressed by the picture in the National Museum, *Policarpa Salavarrieta marcha al suplicio.*

According to Botero, the deformation based on rotundity derives from his wish to create more sensuality, to obtain a greater voluptuousness in the form so that it reaches out to the spectator and he feels pleasure when it strikes his gaze. Botero speaks of the origin of the pleasure one feels when one looks at a picture: "for me it resides in the exaltation of life that is

12 Araújo de Vallejo, Emma (compiler). *Marta Traba*. Bogotá, Museo de Arte Moderno de Bogotá, Planeta Editorial Colombiana S. A., 1984, pag. 48.

13 Araújo de Vallejo, Emma (compiler). *Marta Traba*. Bogotá, Museo de Arte Moderno, Planeta Colombiana Editorial, 1984, pag. 52.

14 Casciero de Sanjurjo, Annick. "Botero. La magia de la realidad" (Botero: the magic of reality), *El Tiempo*, Bogotá, 9 December 1979.

produced by the sensuality of the forms."[15] It must be recalled here that Botero lived in Fiesole, the Italian city where Berenson perfected the theory of tactile values, in which art appears as "an intensifier of life": "That landscape with a little hill is another way of expressing the freedom to fix the proportionality of my elements, just as the 13th and 14th century painters did. In addition, the little mountains in the background transmit a certain sensuality to the earth, to the soil, with which another difficult problem is resolved."[16]

7. The local

Despite having left his birthplace at the age of 18 and having lived outside of his country since 1960, Botero has continued to nourish himself on his provincial roots.

> Thanks to the evocative force that emanates from his images, a whole world – true and false, real and fictitious – is rescuscitated and transmuted into art. In Marinilla (where he spent his childhood), "the atmosphere was very Colombian, the roofs, the houses, just as they are in my pictures. That small city, the cities of the petty bourgeoisie of that epoch – it is from there that my subjects come."[17]

When one observes the *Colombiana* (Colombian Woman) (1983), there are diverse points of interest: her physical type; the roundness of the wrist, simply suggested by the black line of the watchband; but above all, your attention is drawn to the packet of *Pielroja* cigarettes – made of tobacco from Antioquia –; and the design of the packet, by another artist of Antioquia, the cartoonist Ricardo Rendón (1894-1931).

It is not only the objects which appear in his works that are evocative but also the urban and rural landscape, like the rooftops of Cajicá, the town in the savanna region around Bogotá where he has his summer house and which he recalls in his work *Los techos* (1979). When he paints a still life like *Mesa de cocina* (1983), the piece of furniture is placed in a room whose door opens onto the street of a typical Colombian town: "in all of my painting," the artist says, "you

reencounter a world that I knew in my youth in provincial Latin America. It is a kind of nostalgia that has turned into the main theme of my work."[18]

That is how he handles the architecture of the houses and churches of Antioquia and the patriotic holidays seen in his work. In *20 de julio* (1984), which refers to the day on which Colombians commemorate the outbreak of their Independence movement, the subject matter revolves around the activities that characterize the celebration of a national holiday: flags on the houses rippling in the wind, people dressed in their best clothes and the atmosphere of fiesta. Also present are the typical brothels of the region, the bowls of tropical fruits, the families in their Sunday best who crowd his works.

8. Humor

The exaggeration of certain elements enables him to create a special iconography. Annick Sanjurjo writes: "his painting is not a caricature, nor pure irony, nor wounding sarcasm. It is pure reality dissolved into the magic prism of the recollection of the adult who was a child, adolescent and young man in a small valley of a vast region of Latin America."[19]

This humor is found in his reinterpretations of the history of art, like the giant madame Rubens with such short arms, and his way of reworking genres like landscape and still life. In his work *Árbol* (1979), the big branches reach out to cover nearly the whole surface of the picture and the volume is given by the foliage. These elements contrast with the diminutive size of the fruits and the celestial blue of the sky, almost flat, with lengthened white clouds. In the combination of these elements one observes the humor which the painter gives to such a simple subject.

> When you are in Colombia, when you are in Bogotá, you become aware of that which is difficult to understand somewhere else, in Europe or America. The personages, the chronicles of daily life, the moods, are closely related to the ceramics and artworks of the pre-Columbian civilizations.[20]

[15] Ibid.

[16] Von Bonin, Wibke (director). "Reportaje para la televisión alemana" (Story for German television), *El Tiempo*, Bogotá, 1972.

[17] Vargas Llosa, Mario. *Botero*. *Dibujos y acuarelas* (Botero: drawings and watercolors) New York, William Gellender, 1985.

[18] Gianadda, Leonor. *Peintures, dessins et scultures*. Martigny (Switzerland), Fundación Pierre Gianadda, 1990.

[19] Casciero de Sanjurjo, Annick. Op. cit.

[20] Sgarvi, Vittorio. "El nuevo mundo de Botero" (The new world of Botero), *El Tiempo*, Bogotá, 28 July 1991.

July 20th (detail)
(20 de Julio)
1984
Oil on canvas
191 x 144 cm

9. The three dimensions

With *La naranja* (1977), the immense orange that overlays and stretches the limits of the canvas and has become an icon of the National Museum, the antecedents of Botero the sculptor are revealed. It coincides with the affirmation of his leaning towards sculpture in 1970. The point of making this work the backdrop of the Botero gallery in the National Museum is to evoke his arrival at real volume. It may be that his treatment of still lifes is the first step on his path to sculpture. He himself declared: "all of my works are still lifes."[21] "The sculptor´s talent gives life to the flat surface of the pictures and confers on them an unexpected illusion of relief. The spectator lets himself be enveloped in this charming vision where seriousness coexists with humor, without knowing for certain whether the painter is having fun or provoking him to reflect on things."[22]

In the still lifes, the painter seeks the essential and this leads him to the simplicity of the bronze or the marble.

10. The Violence

Botero had dealt with the subject of war in 1973, in a single work that was extensively commented on by the renowned Italian writer Alberto Moravia:

> In a round heap are mixed in bulk all of the personages of Botero: the soldiers with their caps, the priests with their ankle-length dress, the lawyers with their robes, the women with their brassieres and panties, the children with their little suits of clothes–all obese as is customary and all with their eyes closed and their rostrums bloodied. Above them, as though it were flying over a pile of corpses on a battlefield, is a great flag: here and there you catch glimpses of social and family life: altar candles, clothes, bank notes, etc, etc. They are all dead and of this there is no doubt...[23]

What the bishops who are heaped together into a mountain of fat bodies died of has never been explained, but we do know of his interest in real-life violence, of local crimes, like those portrayed in *Doctor Mata*, *Teresita la descuartizada* (Teresita the woman cut into pieces) – events that were widely covered on the crime page of *El Tiempo* newspaper – and *El asesinato de Rosa Calderón* (The murder of Rosa Calderón, 1970). The crime committed by Doctor Mata ("Doctor Kill", from his real name, Nepomuceno Matallana) took place in the very year when Botero went to live in Bogotá, 1951, and the violence and greed behind this murder must have impressed him, because he dealt with these subjects in pictures that were done a decade later. *Teresita la descuartizada* (Teresa Buitrago de Lamarca) was another crime that drew the attention of the painter. The victim was a prostitute, with a violent temperament, who was killed in 1949 by her husband. Her body was quartered and put into suitcases. Botero treated these incidents in great detail.

Although he subsequently returned to the subject sporadically, with works like *Cazador (guerrillero)* (Hunter - guerrilla soldier, 1988) and *La guerrilla de Eliseo Velázquez* (the Eliseo Velázquez guerrilla band), it was only in 1999 that he began to show a strong interest in recreating the dramatic situation of the country. With his portrait of the head of the FARC guerrilla army *Tirofijo* ("Sureshot", the nickname for Manuel Marulanda Vélez, 1999), he began a series which paints and draws real episodes, but this time they have more to do with political than criminal violence.

These subjects, which are so recent that there is no historical perspective on them and they still touch open wounds, have produced diverse reactions. It is necessary to understand that violence also forms part of the history of art, as the artist himself points out:

> I was against the kind of art that becomes a witness to its times in order to serve as a weapon. But in view of the magnitude of the drama that Colombia is experiencing, there came a moment when I felt a moral obligation to leave a testimony about such an irrational period of our history.[24]

The National Museum, in accordance with the wishes of the artist, will hang the 48 works in its history gallery, as a testimony to the events that are now taking place in the country.

[21] Cau, Jean. "L'explotion Botero", *Paris Match*, N.º 2132, April 5, 1990.

[22] Gianadda, Leonor. Op. cit.

[23] Moravia, Alberto. "Elefantes que sonríen" (Elephants who smile), *Lecturas Dominicales*, El Tiempo, December, 1980.

[24] Botero, Fernando. "Con dolor de patria" (With patriotic sorrow), *Revista Diners*, March 2001, pag. 24.

Coconut
(Coco)
1951
Oil on canvas
115 x 95 cm
On permanent loan from the
Ministry of Education

Women doing their hair
(Mujeres peinándose / El peinador)
1953
Oil on canvas
118 x 93,5 cm
On permanent loan from the
Ministry of Education

**Girl
(Muchacha)**
1954
Oil on canvas
98,7 x 78,8 cm

"… I paint in a Colombian way. The truth is that painting the landscapes and

people of Colombia is inborn for me, since it is what I have painted all my life."

FERNANDO BOTERO

Counterpoint
(Contrapunto)
1957
Oil on canvas
110 x 127 cm

Dead Bishops
(Obispos muertos)
1958
Oil on canvas
167 x 195 cm

Sunflowers
(Los girasoles)
Ca. 1959
Oil on canvas
169,5 x 167,2 cm

"I believe that to do something for our country, you do not have to wait until things get better: instead, there is an urgent need to do something that might perhaps speed up the process of returning to normality. That is, I don't believe that you must wait until everything is well in order to make a gesture for your country, but you should it now, at this moment, when it most needs it."

FERNANDO BOTERO

El niño de Vallecas
(after Velázquez´s famous portrait of the
court dwarf Francisco Lezcano)
1959
Oil on canvas
127 x 114,5 cm

91

Guitar lesson
(Lección de guitarra)
1960
Oil on canvas
191 x 246,3 cm

Archdiabolimachy
(Arzodiablomaquia)
1960
Oil on canvas
190,5 x 284,8 cm

Narrative of the life of a saint
(Narrativa de la vida de un santo)
Ca. 1960 / 1
Oil on canvas
33 x 128 cm

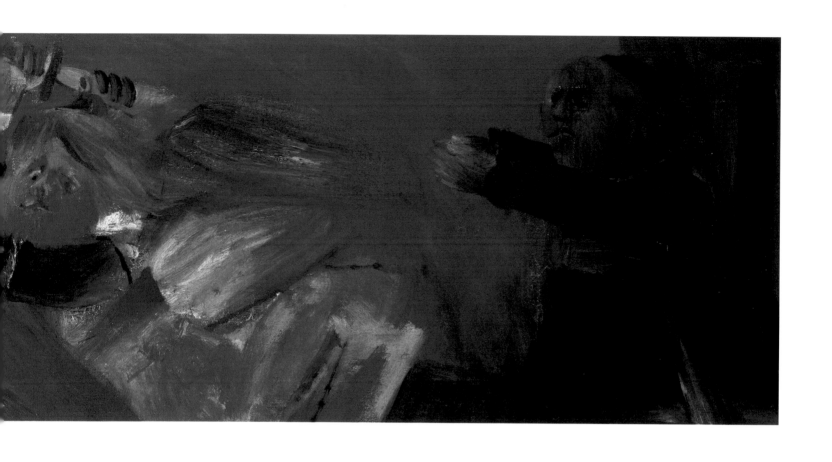

Pedro
1971
Oil on canvas
122 x 90,5 cm

Orange
(Naranja)
1977
Oil on canvas
224,5 x 195 cm

Forest
(El bosque)
1979
Oil on canvas
233 x 309 cm

Tree
(El árbol)
1979
Oil on canvas
260 x 309 cm

Roofs
(Los techos)
1979
Oil on canvas
246 x 309 cm

The street
(La calle)
1980
Oil on canvas
218,5 x 180,5 cm

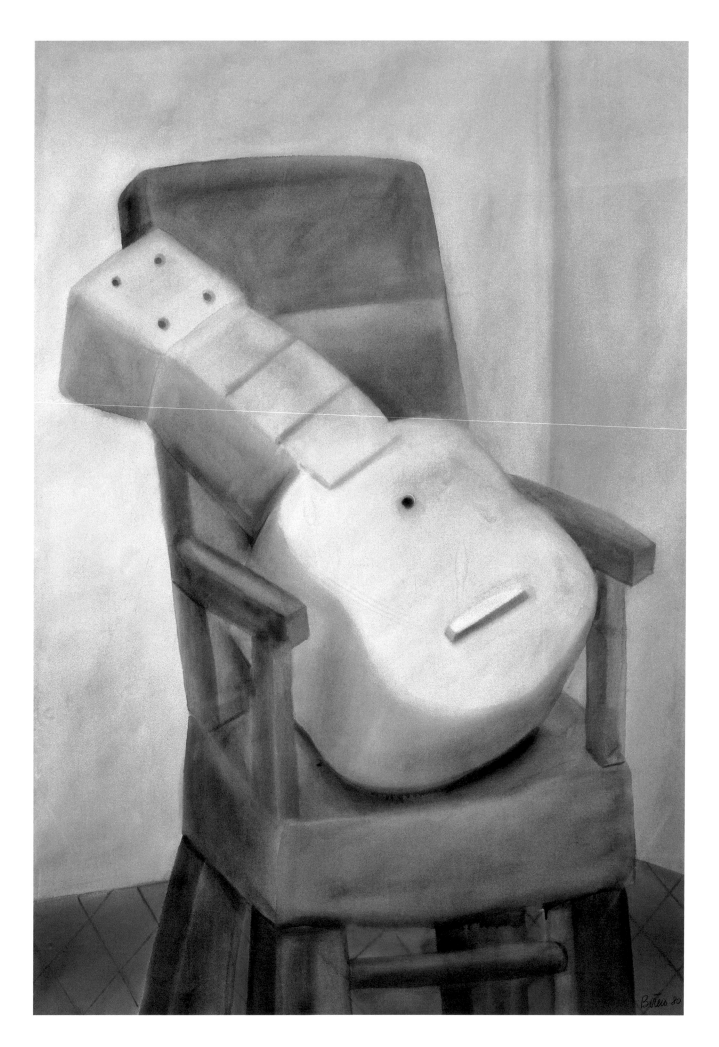

Chair with guitar
(Silla con guitarra)
1980
Watercolor
162,4 x 114,5 cm

Flower vase
(Florero)
1980
Watercolor
200,4 x 115,5 cm

Still life
(Naturaleza muerta)
1983
Oil on canvas
128,5 x 164 cm

Kitchen table
(Mesa de cocina)
1983
Oil on canvas
191 x 126 cm

"… As everyone knows I am very Colombian, even in the way I talk, and I have a profound love for my country and I am very concerned about everything that happens there; I keep up with things… all my life I have been very well informed about the things that go on there and I am very distressed about the crisis that we are living through, but I have a great hope that things will change and get better."

FERNANDO BOTERO

Colombian woman
(Colombiana)
1983
Oil on canvas
115,5 x 90,5 cm

July 20th
(20 de Julio)
1984
Oil on canvas
191 x 144 cm

Biography

1932. On April 19 Fernando Botero was born in Medellín, capital of the Department of Antioquia in Colombia, in the home of David Botero (1895-1936), an energetic businessman who traveled around the neighboring provinces on horseback – the only available means of transport in that period – and Flora Angulo de Botero (1898-1972), a creative woman known for her skill at handicrafts. Flora´s two sisters, the Angulo aunts, lived there and had a special place in the painter´s heart. He has two brothers, Juan David (1928) and Rodrigo (1936).

1938-1949. He studied at the Ateneo Antioqueño primary school and attended the Boliviarana high school. When he was 12, his uncle Joaquín sent him to a bullfighters school in the Macarena bull ring of Medellín. He showed his early drawings at the store of don Rafael Arango, where tickets for the bullfights were sold. The first work he sold was priced at two pesos. On weekends he would climb the hills surrounding Medellín to paint and draw. He admired pre-Columbian art, the baroque style of the city´s churches and artists like José Clemente Orozco. It was in this epoch that he discovered Dalí and Picasso. In 1948 two of his watercolors were included in a collective show at the Fine Arts Institute of Medellín.

1948-1950. He paid for his studies in the Liceo San José and the Normal de Marinilla high schools with drawings he did for the Sunday supplement of *El Colombiano* newspaper, but he was fired for being a non-conformist after writing an article on Picasso. He designed the stage sets for the work *Ardiente Oscuridad* (Burning Darkness), by Bueno Vallejo, which was presented by the Lope de Vega theater group of Spain, which was touring Colombia. He took part in the "Intellectual Panorama" radio program, where the young intellectuals of the country debated with the traditionalists. He moved to Bogotá, joined the artistic avant-garde and participated in collective exhibitions.

1951. He held his first one-man show in Bogotá. The painter Ignacio Gómez Jaramillo, the poet León de Greiff and the writer Jorge Zalamea became interested in his work. He traveled to Tolú, a village on the Caribbean coast of Colombia. There, he stayed at the boarding house of Isolinia García and paid for his lodging with a mural. He wound up painting on some sheets which were embroidered with the monogram of his mother. At that time he was influenced by Gauguin and the pink and blue periods of Picasso.

1952. He returned to Bogotá, held an exhibition and sold all of his pictures. He won the second prize in the *IX Annual Salon of Colombian Artists.* The Eddy Torres publishing house published a monograph on his work, the first ever done, when he was barely 20 years old. From the Colombian port of Buenaventura he traveled on the Italian ship *Usodimare* to Barcelona and from there went to Madrid, where he studied for a time in the Academia de San Fernando. In El Prado museum he discovered Velázquez and Goya. He painted copies of such works to supplement his budget.

1953-1954. He spent the summers in Paris, where he studied the great painters in the Louvre. He traveled to Italy, where he enrolled at the San Marcos

Academy and attended Robert Longhi´s lectures on the history of art. "I consider my years in Florence as the most important in my training," he later remarked. He became familiar with the Italian Renaissance art of Rome, Florence, Venice, Sienna and Ravenna and deepened his knowledge of 14th century Italian art, the main inspiration of his painting. He read Berenson and learned about tactile values and the representation of volumes. He visited the most important frescoes of Italy and devoted himself to studying their techniques. He appropriated the complete plasticity that characterizes the work of such artists as Piero della Francesca, Paolo Uccello, Titian, Giotto and Masaccio. Through this research, "I gradually acquired a greater clarity about what the space and the volume were trying to tell me. It heightened my desire for the enormous, the strong and the monumental".

1955. He returned to Bogotá and held an exhibition of the works he had done in Italy, which were not received with much enthusiasm. He married Gloria de Antei.

1956. He settled in Mexico, where he studied pre-Columbian art and the work of the Mexican muralists, which attracted him because they seemed to express the essence of the Latin American spirit. It was when he was painting the work *Naturaleza Muerta, con Mandolina* (Still life with Mandolin) that he discovered the possibility of increasing the volume of the forms. "One day, when I was completely exhausted, I made a small mark in the center of a mandolin that I had been drawing". This small circle gave the instrument the solidity that would wind up in his encounter with the "Boterian" proportion. "It was like going through a door to enter another room". He exhibited for the first time in the U.S., as part of a collective show in the Houston Museum of Fine Arts. His son Fernando was born.

1957. He traveled to New York with 200 dollars in his pocket and settled in the Village. "I was attracted by the energy of the city and the high standards that were demanded in a place that had an avalanche of talent". He became interested in De Kooning and Dubuffet, for their generous use of gesture and material. The Pan American Union sponsored his first one-man show in the United States, held in Washington, D.C. He returned to Bogotá, where he won the second prize in the *X Annual Salon of Colombian Artists.*

1958. He was appointed art professor at the School of Fine Arts at the National University of Colombia in Bogotá. He won the first prize in the *XI Annual Salon of Colombian Artists,* with the work *La cámara nupcial (Homenaje a Mantegna) No.1.* (The bridal chamber- Homage to Mantegna, No. 1). He opened his first one-man exhibition in the Gres Gallery of Washington, which was a success. His work was chosen for the XXIX Venice Biennial. His daughter Lina was born.

1959. He represented Colombia in the V Biennial of São Paulo, Brazil, together with the artists Enrique Grau, Alejando Obregón and Eduardo Ramírez Villamizar.

1960. He painted a fresco for the Banco Central Hipotecario (bank) in Medellín. His son Juan Carlos was born. He was chosen to represent Colombia at the II Biennial of Mexico: his participation roused so much controversy that, with the rest of his colleagues who had been chosen, he refused to participate in the Biennial. Instead, they organized a show in Bogotá entitled *Paintings and Reliefs (by the painters self-excluded from the II Biennial of Mexico).* He returned to New York, where he obtained the prize for Colombian artists in the *Guggenheim International Award 1960.* He went through a very difficult period of his career: abstract art was at its peak and if you were not an abstractionist, you were not a painter. "For years I believed in myself and in what I was doing, despite the most horrible criticism. In *Art News* magazine they said, for example, that my figures were ´fetuses of the union between Mussolini and an idiot peasant woman `. *Art Magazine* treated me better: it said that my painting was a ´a monument to stupidity´. And these were the critics who spoke of my painting in terms of my work, because the rest spoke of Botero's 'cartoons'. In the midst of this whole tempest, I kept my faith in myself, in my work". He and Gloria de Antei separated.

1961. The New York Museum of Modern Art acquired his work *Mona Lisa at the age of twelve* (1958).

1962. Held a one-man show at the Gres Gallery of Chicago.

1963. The New York Museum of Modern Art exhibited his *Mona Lisa at the age of twelve* at the same time that Leonardo da Vinci's *Mona Lisa* was on view in the Metropolitan Museum.

1964. He won the second prize in the first "Intercol Salon for Young Artists", held at the Bogotá Museum of Modern Art. Pictures done at this time, like *The Pinzón Family*, show that he had perfected the consistent and controlled touch he needed for the attainment of pictorial mastery. "What interests me is to heighten the sensuality of the form associated with tactile values". He married Cecilia Zambrano.

1966. He held a solo exhibition in Baden-Baden and Hanover, Germany. His first exhibition in a U.S. museum – a retrospective – was held at the Milwaukee Art Center. *Time* magazine published a critical piece praising his work.

1967-1968. He divided his time between Bogotá, New York and Rome. In Nuremberg and Munich he studied the works of Dürer. He painted his *Durerboteros*. He became interested in Manet and Bonnard, although he affirmed his Latin American roots. "I want to be capable of painting everything, even Marie Antoinette and Louis XV, but with the hope that everything I do will be impregnated with the soul of Latin America".

1969. He exhibited in the Center for Inter-American Relations, New York and opened his first solo exhibition in Paris, at the Claude Bernard Gallery.

1970. A retrospective showing of 80 of his works was held in Baden-Baden and then traveled to four museums in Germany. He exhibited at the Hanover Gallery of London. "This was the time when many galleries began to get interested in my work". His son Pedro was born.

1971. He moved his studio in New York to Thirtieth street. He rented an apartment in the Boulevard du Palais, in Paris and opened a studio in Bogotá.

1972. First individual exhibition at the Marlborough Gallery of New York.

1973. Moved to Paris. Earliest sculptures. First retrospective in Bogotá.

1974. Exhibited in Hanover, Medellín and Zurich. His four year-old son Pedro was killed in a car accident in Spain in which Botero was injured.

1975. Exhibited in Caracas, Rotterdam, New York, Toronto and Montreal. He and Cecilia Zambrano separated.

1976. Exhibited in Paris. Held a retrospective in Caracas, where the President of Venezuela awarded him the "Andrés Bello" Order. Exhibited in Washington and Bogotá. Worked exclusively on sculpture. "Sculpture is a natural consequence of my work as a painter, where volume has always been present".

1977. Awarded the Colombian government's highest distinction, *La Cruz de Boyacá* (Cross of Boyacá), with the rank of Officer. To honor the memory of his dead son, the Pedrito Botero hall was opened in the Museum of Antioquia, to which he donated 16 works. First solo exhibition of sculptures at the Paris International Art Fair (FIAC). Worked on the *Margarita* series, inspired by Velázquez.

1978. Moved his Paris studio to a part of the old seat of the Académie Julian. He joined his life to that of the Greek artist Sophia Vari, an outstanding painter, sculptress and jewelry designer.

1979. First big retrospective exhibition in the U.S., in the Hirshhorn Museum of Washington. Traveling exhibitions in Belgium, Norway and Sweden.

1980. Moved to a house and sculpture studio in Pietrasanta, Italy. *Vogue* magazine commissioned him to paint a series of women dressed by the great fashion designers. Exhibited in Basle. Published articles and illustrations in Bogotá's *El Tiempo* newspaper.

1981. Retrospectives in Tokyo and Osaka. Exhibition of watercolors and drawings in Rome, with an essay in the catalogue by Alberto Moravia. Exhibited in New York, San Francisco and Chicago.

1982. Exhibited in Boston and New York, the latter show traveled to Houston, Chicago, Philadelphia and Boston.

1983. Exhibited in Basle. Showed his most recent work in London.

1984. Sculpture exhibition in Chicago and New York, exhibition of drawings and sculptures in Ithaca, and of sculptures in Utica, Scranton and Lafayette. Donated a sculpture hall to the Museum of Antioquia and 18 pictures to the Colombian National Library in Bogotá. In this period he mainly painted bullfighting scenes. "I have dared to paint the bullfight because I know the subject very well. You cannot paint something if there is no relation between the subject matter and your soul. This gives one a certain moral authority. This theme surges from my heart, my life".

1985. Exhibited his large-format sculptures and a series of bullfighting paintings at the Marlborough Gallery of New York. Held exhibitions in Coral Gables and the Ponce Museum, in San Juan, Puerto Rico.

1986. Retrospective in Munich, Bremen and Frankfurt. Also exhibited in Albany, Tokyo and Caracas.

1987. Retrospective in the "Reina Sofía" Art Center in Madrid. Exhibited in Bogotá and Hamburg. Exhibited his series *La Corrida* (The Bullfight) in Milan.

1988. Presented the series *La Corrida* in Naples and Palermo.

1989. Presented the series *La Corrida* in Coro, Caracas and Mexico City. Exhibited his sculptures in the Los Angeles Art Fair and in New York and Mexico City.

1990. Exhibited in Belgium; retrospective in Switzerland; recent sculptures in New York.

1991. Exhibited in Berlin, Florence and Tokyo. In Rome exhibited pictures, drawing and sculptures on *La Corrida*. His sculptures were shown at the Biennial of Monte Carlo.

1992. Exhibition in Seville and retrospective in Vienna. Monumental sculptures in Monte Carlo. Bullfighting paintings in Paris, together with recent works on paper and small-format sculptures. 32 of his monumental sculptures are displayed on the Champs-Élysées in Paris. On that occasion, the French President Jacques Chirac remarked: "Botero is, in fact, the link between two continents that are different and complementary at the same time, between two worlds: that of the Western masters and that of the Latin American tradition".

1993. Exhibited at the Palace of the Popes in Avignon, the Pushkin Museum in Moscow and the Hermitage Museum in Saint Petersburg. His monumental sculptures were displayed along Park Avenue in New York.

1994. Retrospective in Helsinki. Exhibited in New York, Chicago and Fort Lauderdale. Exhibition at the National Museum of Fine Arts, Buenos Aires, together with a showing of his large sculptures in the gardens of the museum. His monumental sculptures are displayed on the Paseo de Recolectos, Madrid.

1995. Exhibitions in Belgium, Paris and Beverly Hills. He opened a traveling show in Japan.

1996. His work continued to travel round the world: Jerusalem, New York, Washington, Berlin, Caracas, Kyongju. Designed the sets and costumes for Donizetti's *Fille du Régiment* a co-production of the Montecarlo, Geneva and Düsseldorf opera companies.

1997. Exhibitions in Santiago (Chile), Rome, Madrid and Lugano.

1998. Exhibited his monumental sculptures in the Plaza do Comercio in Lisbon. His work was shown in São Paulo and Basle.

1999. In an unprecedented recognition, Botero was invited to exhibit in the Piazza della Signoria, in Florence, an honor which no other painter has received to the present day. He simultaneously exhibited paintings and small-format sculptures in the Hall of Arms of the Palazzo Vecchio.

2000. Donated an important collection of 85 of his own works and 21 by international artists to Medellín, and 136 of his own works and 52 pictures from his private collection to Bogotá. All of these works were exhibited at the Fundación Santander Central Hispano, Madrid. He also exhibited in Tel Aviv and Pietrasanta.

2001. Exhibited at the Bricherasio Palace in Turin. Opened an exhibition on the 50 years of his artistic life in Mexico City. Exhibited his work in Paris and New York.

2002. Inaugurated an exhibition of his work in Dinard.

2003. His monumental sculptures were exhibited in the Ducal Palace and along the Grand Canal of Venice. Opened a retrospective in the Hague.

2004. Donated the series of paintings on the theme of the violence in Colombia to the National Museum of Colombia, in Bogotá.